Hello!
I am a chicken.

Chickens can live for about 5 to 10 years.

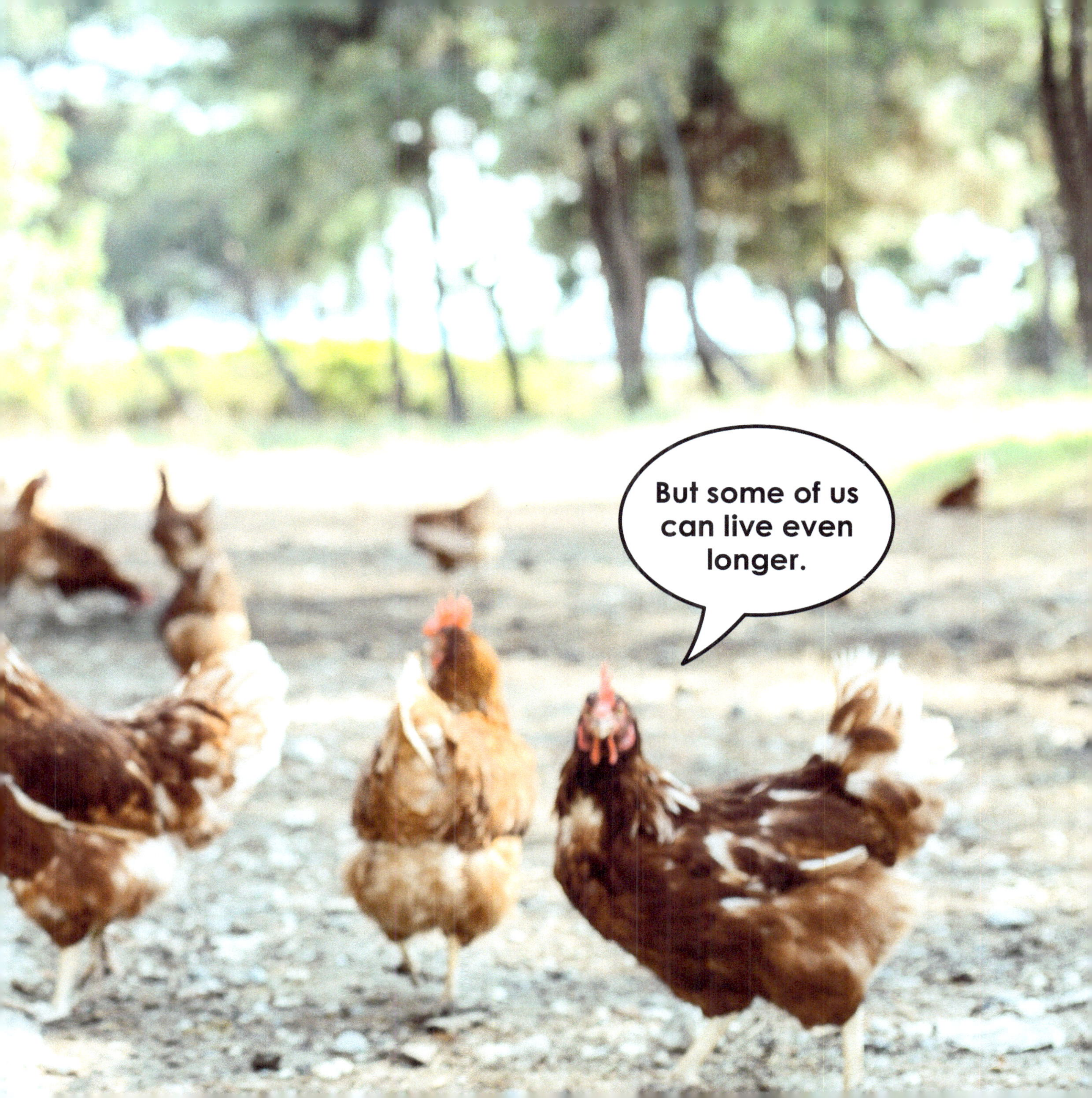
But some of us can live even longer.

Chickens are omnivores.

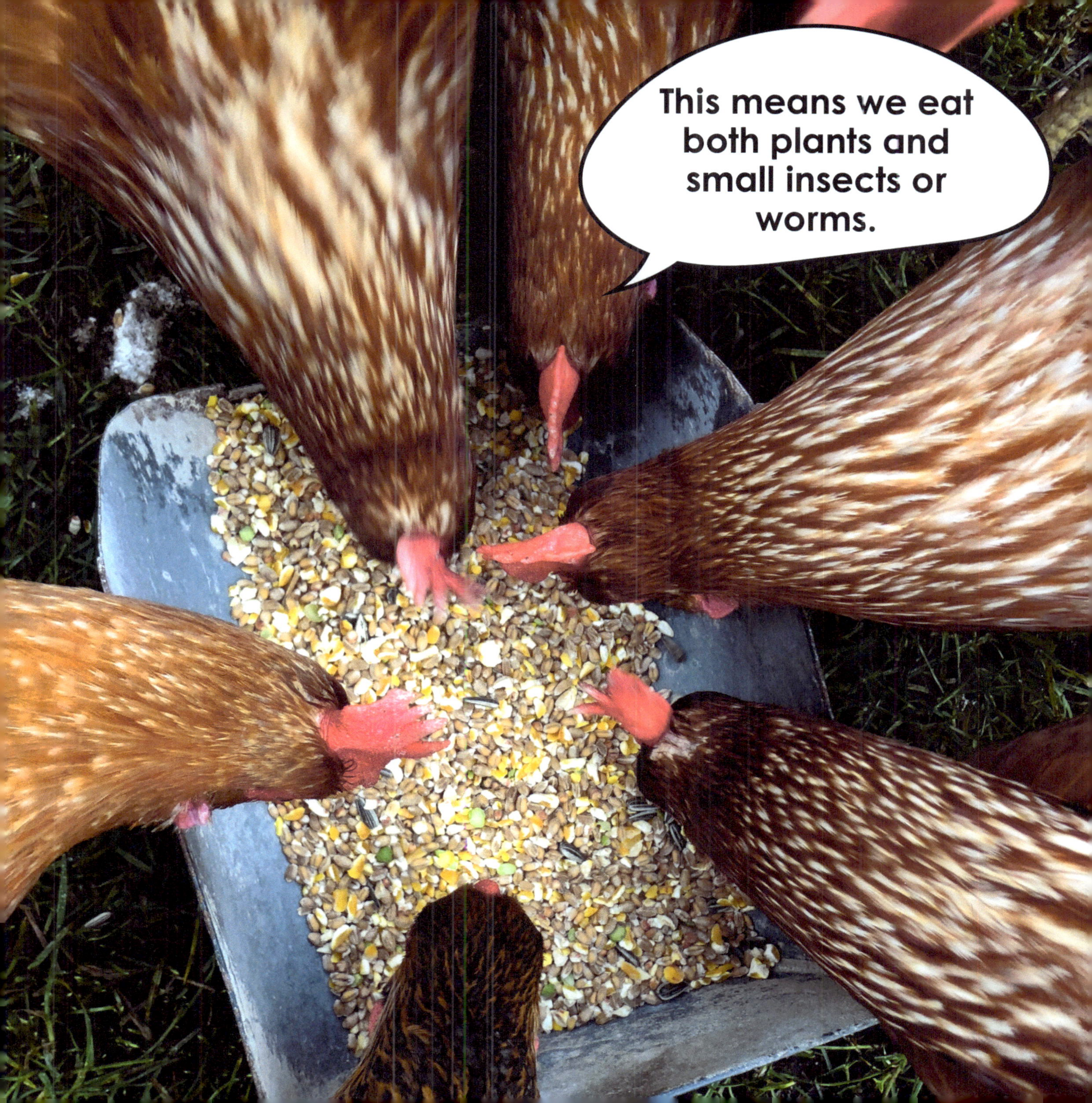
This means we eat both plants and small insects or worms.

Chickens eggs can be white, brown, or even blue or green.

The color of our eggs depends on our breed.

Laying an egg takes about 25 hours.

A group of chickens is called a "flock".

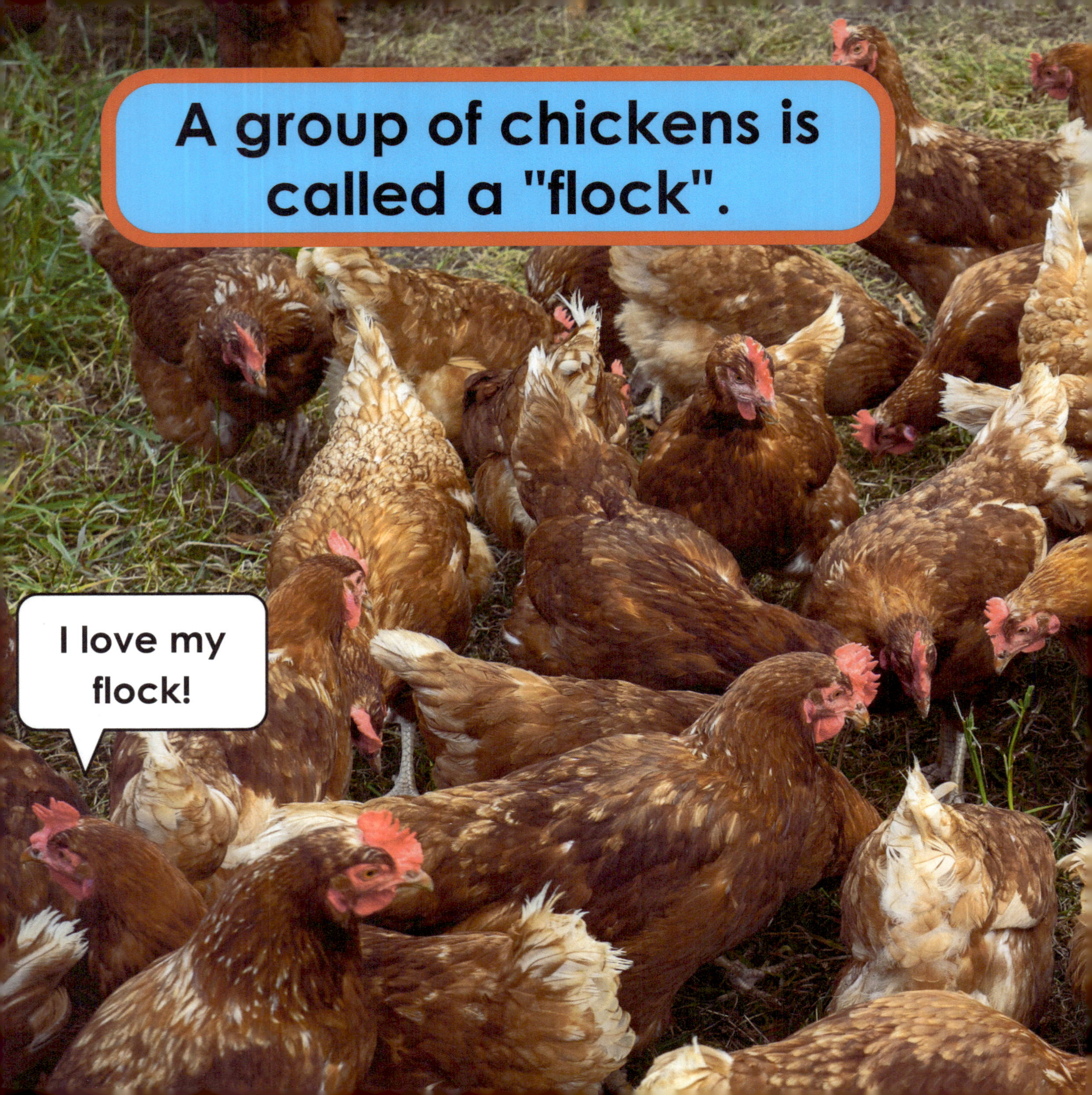

Chickens are social animals.

Roosters are male chickens,
and hens are female chickens.

Chickens have been known to show empathy and care for sick or injured flock members.

Please let me know if you need anything.

Chickens have wings, but they are not very good at flying.

I can fly!

...but not far.

Chickens can fly up to 330 feet (100 m).

I have a good sense of smell.

Chickens can even smell things underwater.

There are many different breeds of chickens, each can look very different.

Chickens come in many colors like white, black, brown, and even blue or green.

Chickens can run up to 9 miles (14 km) per hour .

We can be hard to catch.

Chickens are good at balancing.

Chickens have been trained to be around humans for thousands of years.

Across the world chickens lay over one billion eggs every year.

I'll take good care of you.

Chickens can be used as therapy animals to help people feel better.

You need to take good care of us.

Chickens can be good pets.

Chickens have taste buds on the roof of their mouth.

They help me enjoy my food.

Chickens take dust baths to keep their feathers clean and remove parasites.

I just love a good bath.

Baby chickens are called "chicks."

Mama.

Chickens parents protect their eggs and chicks.

Chickens can see colors, but they see them differently than humans do.

Chickens have special parts in their eyes that helps them find their way.

I know where I am going.

Chickens have a good memory.

Chickens can remember and recognize up to 100 other chickens and humans.

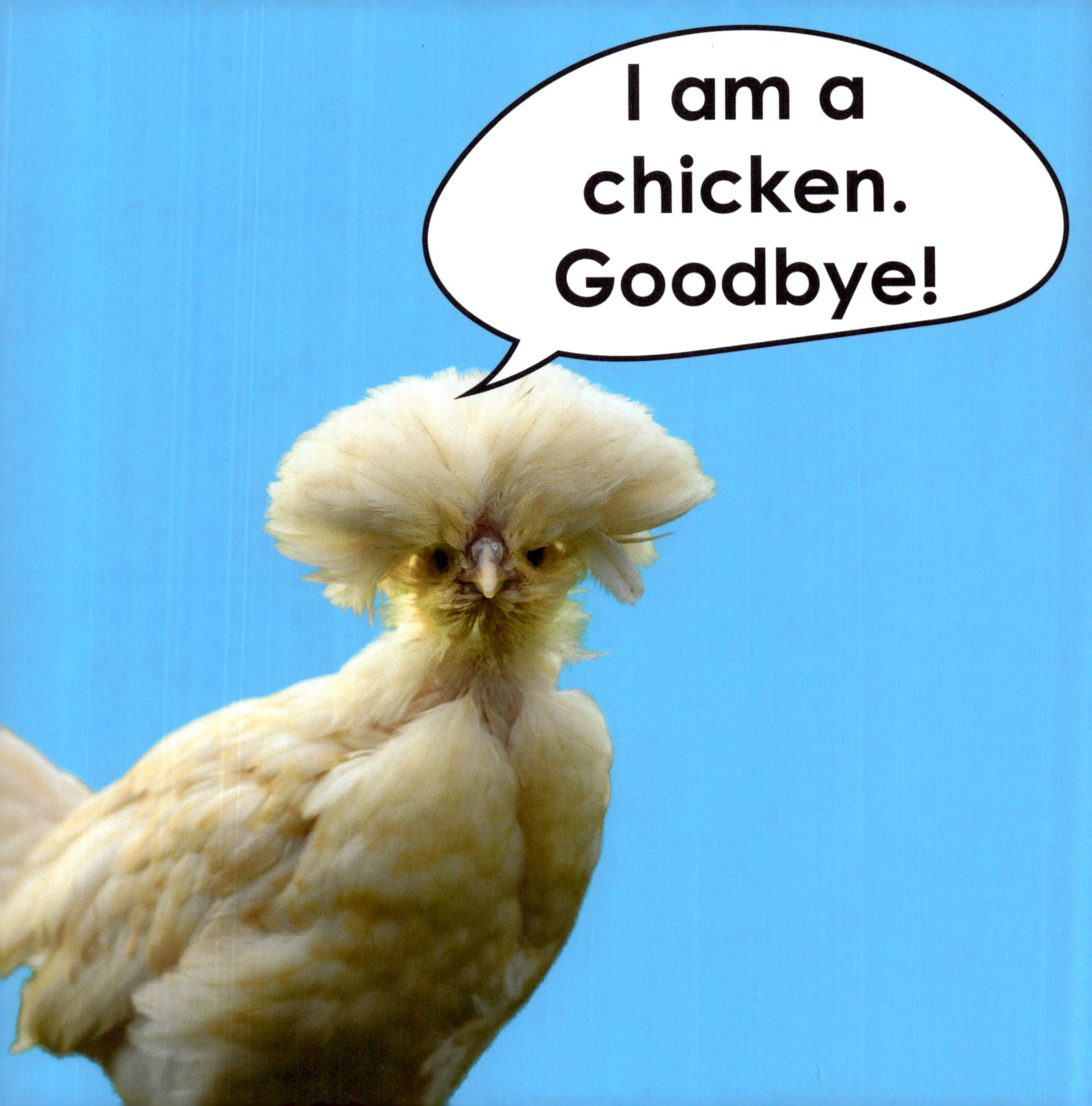
I am a chicken. Goodbye!

Want more?

Hello parents!

scan here

Visit us to find out about new releases and **FREE** offers. We'll let you know when we have a new release coming out and how you can get it for FREE.
And you can cast your vote for what book we make next!

ActiveBrainsBooks.com

or visit here

scan here

Let us know what you think. As an independent publisher, your honest reviews mean a lot to us and our business. We'd love to hear from you!

amazon.com/review/create-review/

or visit here

FOLLOW US on Amazon.

amazon.com/author/activebrainsbooks

ActiveBrainsBooks.com

ACTIVE BRAINS

www.ingramcontent.com/pod-product-compliance
Lightning Source LLC
Chambersburg PA
CBHW042056040426
42447CB00003B/250